It's a Girl's Word!

Move to the head of the class
with vocabulary to help you pass!

by Trula Magruder

★ AmericanGirl®

Published by American Girl Publishing
Copyright © 2013 by American Girl

Questions or comments? Call 1-800-845-0005, visit **americangirl.com,** or write to Customer Service, American Girl, 8400 Fairway Place, Middleton, WI 53562-0497.

Printed in China
13 14 15 16 17 18 19 20 LEO 10 9 8 7 6 5 4 3 2 1

All American Girl and Innerstar Universtiy marks are trademarks of American Girl.

Editorial Development: Trula Magruder
Art Direction and Design: Lisa Wilber
Production: Tami Kepler, Judith Lary, Kendra Schluter
Illustrations: Thu Thai at Arcana Studios

INNERSTARU.COM

Dear Reader,

At Innerstar University, an **imaginary,** one-of-a-kind school, you can live with your friends in a dorm called Brightstar House, where you'll learn to **foster** an **infinite** number of special talents.

For this book, that special talent will be **exposing** and **unraveling** new words. These **ubiquitous** words could be buried under a bed, hung in a closet, or tossed about at school. They'll be silly words, long words, serious words, **unusual** words, foreign words, and words that sound just like what they mean.

You'll also need **expertise** at solving puzzling problems, because one thing is certain: your ISU guides will find themselves caught in **predicaments!** Lucky for you, as you help them out, you'll **expand** your vocabulary *and* have an **amusing** time.

Baffled by a word problem? Peek inside *The Quictionary*! It may help you solve the **lingo-ladened** puzzles—and better understand this letter.

Check your answers, starting on page 72. Then **advance** to www.innerstarU.com for more **intriguing** games.

Your friends at American Girl

Innerstar Guides

Every girl needs a few good friends to help her find her way.

Emmy

A brave girl who loves
swimming and boating

Isabel

A confident girl with
a funky sense of style

Riley

A good sport, on
the field and off

Paige

A nature lover who leads hikes
and campus cleanups

Amber

An animal lover
and a loyal friend

Neely

A creative girl who loves
dance, music, and art

Logan

A super-smart girl
who is curious about
EVERYTHING

Shelby

A kind girl who is there
for her friends—and loves
making NEW friends!

Innerstar U Campus

1. Rising Star Stables
2. Star Student Center
3. Brightstar House
4. Starlight Library
5. Sparkle Studios
6. Blue Sky Nature Center

7. Real Spirit Center
8. Five-Points Plaza
9. Starfire Lake & Boathouse
10. U-Shine Hall
11. Good Sports Center
12. Shopping Square
13. The Market
14. Morningstar Meadow

Table of Contents

Check it out, and then check it off!

Hobby Shop

☐ Craft Laughs 12

☐ Sew Blue 13

☐ Sorts of Sports 14

☐ Dress for Dance 16

☐ Earth Art 18

☐ Bed Boutique 19

☐ Cooking Clues 20

☐ Music Mania 21

☐ Twisted Travelogue 22

☐ Newer Entrepreneur..24

☐ Alien Animals..26

By, Buy, Bye!

☐ Hear Here 28

☐ Double the Fun 30

☐ Too Close for Comfort 32

Onyms Island

☐ Giggles and Groans..34

☐ Camp Weak 36

☐ Logan's Letter..38

☐ Secret Sorry..39

☐ Ta-Ta Tautonyms 40

☐ C U at ISU! 42

☐ Retro Lingo 44

School Studies

☐ Front Office...46

☐ Social Studies: Part 1 48

☐ Social Studies: Part 2 50

☐ Language Arts..52

☐ Art 101..53

☐ Math: Part 1 54

☐ Math: Part 2 56

Sounds Like Onomatopoeia

☐ Ahem, Action! 58

☐ Cackle Cards 60

☐ Ouch!.. 62

☐ Pitter-Patter Pets 64

☐ Clatter Control...................................... 66

Brilliant Briticisms

☐ Needed: Baby-Minder.............................68

☐ Nice Nosh-Up..69

☐ Sleep Gear..70

Answers start on page 72.

Meet Shelby

Work side by side with your Innerstar University guide.

At Innerstar University, you'll spot Shelby right away. She's the girl taking campus photos for the yearbook—so be sure to smile if you see her! And when she's not at the yearbook office, she's exploring new activities.

But Shelby isn't just passionate about activities and the yearbook—she loves offering advice and helping friends. That's why she's been asked to guide this book.

So don't be surprised if you see Shelby pop up to share a nugget-sized tip that will help you on your word journey. Who knows? Maybe one day you, too, will be a student guide on campus . . . and use remarkable words along the way!

Look for my speech bubbles for tips and guidance throughout the book. If you need help with any tricky words in this book, look in "The Quictionary."

Hobby Shop

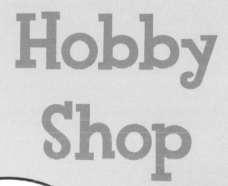

If you play soccer, sporting terms will leap from your lips. If you garden, planting phrases will take root in your sentences. So to expand your vocabulary, try new activities!

Craft Laughs

The crafting club wrote a few jokes to tell at the Sparkle Studios luncheon. Using the word list below, write in each punch line.

collage

crocheters

embroidery floss

varnish

1. Why did the woodworker seem like a ghost?

   Because she liked to _____ into thin air!

2. What do you get when you cross a crafter with a dentist?

   Someone who hands out toothpaste and _____!

3. Where does papier-mâché go to school?

   It attends _____!

4. What crafters tell the best stories?

   _____, because they love a good yarn!

Sew Blue

Emmy loved the cerulean blue dress she saw in Isabel's closet and decided to sew a skirt in the same color. But when she ordered material, she asked for *blue* fabric—she didn't know the word *cerulean*. When a bolt of *navy* arrived, Emmy had to sew a sailing shirt instead. To help with future orders, use the colors listed to label these swatches for Emmy.

burgundy   eggplant   lilac   navy

cerulean   emerald   lime   periwinkle

coral   fuchsia   mahogany   turquoise

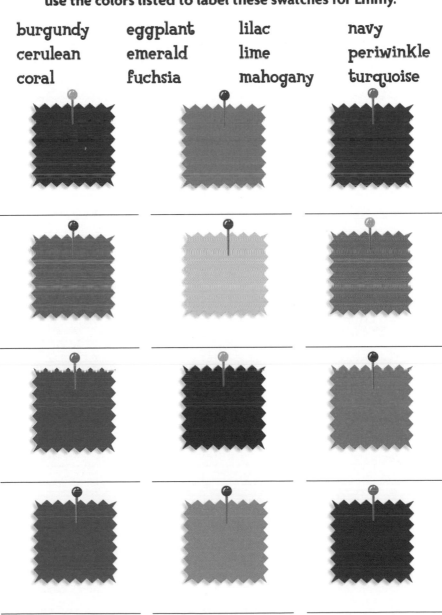

Sorts of Sports

Riley and Emmy have teamed up for a sports-trivia challenge at school, but they need your help. Using the list below, match each word to its definition.

barre	goggles	powder
dismount	hurdles	putter
épée	infield	shuttlecock
goalkeeper	love	spinnaker

Contestants, please name . . .

1. a gymnastics skill used to get off a piece of equipment.

   _____

2. the waist-high horizontal pole ballet dancers use to warm up.

   _____

3. the diamond-shaped area in softball formed by three bases and

   a home plate. _____

4. the official term for badminton's "birdie." _____

5. the golf club used to hit a ball into a hole after it lands on the

   green. _____

6. the snow-skiing term for freshly fallen and fluffy snow.

   _____

7. a tennis term that means "no score." _____

8. the barriers runners jump over in track. _____

9. the largest and most colorful sail used in sailing.

   _____

10. the swimming glasses used to protect eyes from chlorine and to

    see better underwater. _____

11. the dueling sword used in fencing. _____

12. the position of the soccer player who prevents shots from passing

    into the net. _____

Dress for Dance

For a class report, Neely plans to give a slide show on all the dance wear she has in her closet. Write the name of each of her pieces on the correct slide while she practices her speech.

ball gown ♥
ghillies ♥
leotard ♥
petticoat ♥

pointe shoes ♥
tap shoes ♥
tutu ♥
unitard ♥

1. Ball gown

2. Tap Shoes

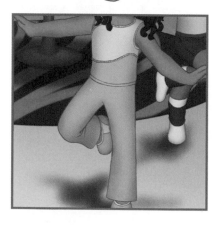

3. unitard

4. Tutu

5. Petticoat

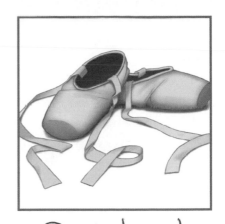

6. Pointe shoes

7. leotard

8. ghillies

Earth Art

Paige made Earth Day necklaces but can't finish them because customers are swarming her craft booth. Follow each necklace string, and write down its beaded word. Then, next to the clasp, write the letter of the message she meant for that necklace.

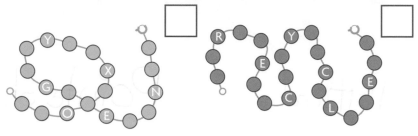

1. _____ 2. _____

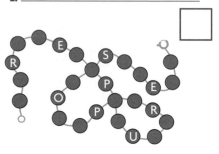 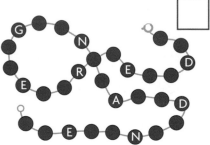

3. _____ 4. _____

A. If you can, use what you have over and over again.

C. Dispose of unwanted items properly to give them a new life.

B. Take a breath, and then help to preserve the gas that supports life on Earth.

D. Don't end a species. Help Earth keep plants and animals alive.

Bed Boutique

Isabel placed bins under her bed to store her extra fashions and furnishings. Write down the correct bin letter next to each item on Isabel's list.

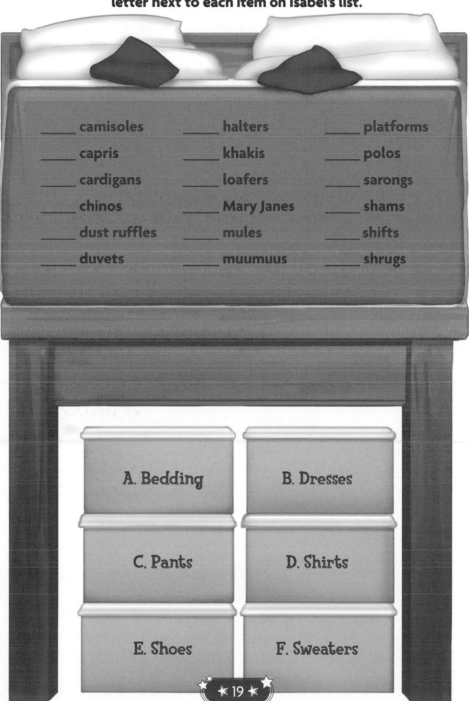

_____ camisoles   _____ halters   _____ platforms

_____ capris   _____ khakis   _____ polos

_____ cardigans   _____ loafers   _____ sarongs

_____ chinos   _____ Mary Janes   _____ shams

_____ dust ruffles   _____ mules   _____ shifts

_____ duvets   _____ muumuus   _____ shrugs

A. Bedding

B. Dresses

C. Pants

D. Shirts

E. Shoes

F. Sweaters

Cooking Clues

For the final project in Logan's cooking class, she threw a dinner party. On the invitation, she created a puzzle to reveal what she's serving. Follow the directions to discover Logan's dish.

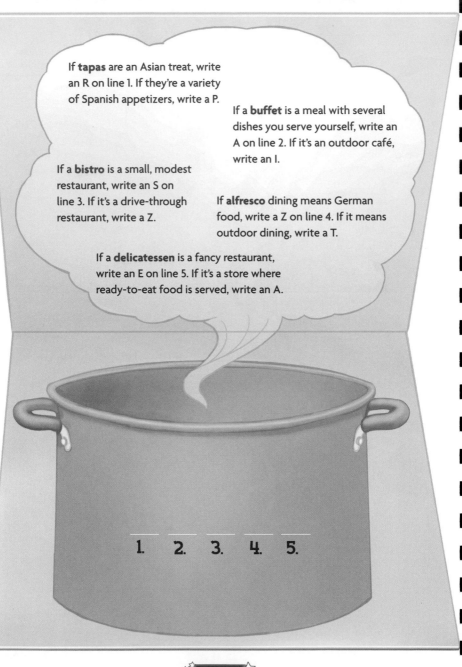

If **tapas** are an Asian treat, write an R on line 1. If they're a variety of Spanish appetizers, write a P.

If a **buffet** is a meal with several dishes you serve yourself, write an A on line 2. If it's an outdoor café, write an I.

If a **bistro** is a small, modest restaurant, write an S on line 3. If it's a drive-through restaurant, write a Z.

If **alfresco** dining means German food, write a Z on line 4. If it means outdoor dining, write a T.

If a **delicatessen** is a fancy restaurant, write an E on line 5. If it's a store where ready-to-eat food is served, write an A.

1. ___ 2. ___ 3. ___ 4. ___ 5. ___

Music Mania

Neely designed music posters for the walls in U-Shine Hall. She created images and sayings but needs to match them up. Write the number of each caption below the poster that it best fits.

1. _____

2. _____

A. Do you know an **alto?**

B. Get set with a **duet!**

3. _____

4. _____

C. Live your **lyrics.**

D. Explore a **score** today.

5. _____

6. _____

E. Sweet 'n' **soprano.**

F. Tra-la-la with a **trio!**

Twisted Travelogue

Paige texted a very *elaborate* e-mail, but it lacked some important details. To see what she's up to, study her message until you've crossed off all but one of the options in each box. We've done 1 4 U!

Friends,

While at the airport, I whizzed through the ~~security check~~ & ran into a girl who lost her paper slip issued at check-in! She's staying in a cheap place 4 students, but plans 2 pay 4 a driver 2 take her 2 a drive-up sleeping place. The person who looks after R needs on the plane told me that he met a teacher on the last flight who lost her government-issued citizenship document on either a boat that carries people and sometimes cars or a boat that uses heated water for power. He said that she had slept in a round tent made of felt and skins! I heard 2 people talking Spanish on the plane—1 from SW North America and 1 from SW Europe. They R staying in a room in a house that serves an AM meal & R taking an underground train 2 get 2 it. Then I heard 2 people speaking French—1 from Paris and 1 from Montreal. So, I made it, but my bags R another story. Time 2 float away!

WBS,
Paige

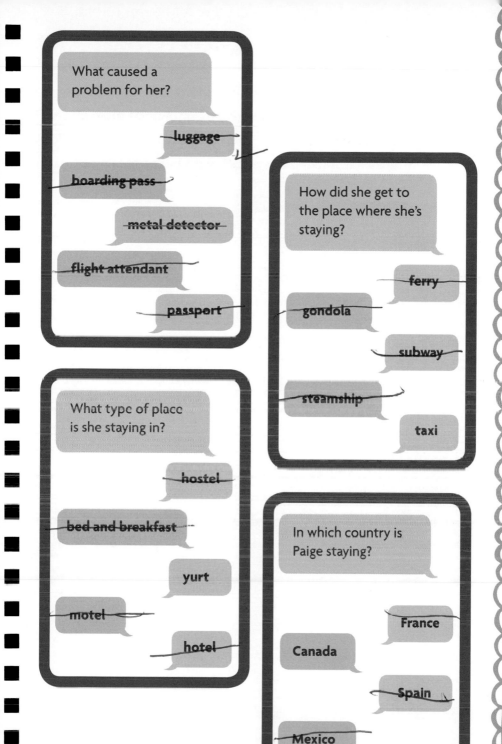

What caused a problem for her?

~~luggage~~

~~boarding pass~~

~~metal detector~~

~~flight attendant~~

passport

How did she get to the place where she's staying?

~~ferry~~

~~gondola~~

~~subway~~

~~steamship~~

taxi

What type of place is she staying in?

~~hostel~~

~~bed and breakfast~~

yurt

~~motel~~

~~hotel~~

In which country is Paige staying?

France

Canada

~~Spain~~

~~Mexico~~

~~Italy~~

★ 23 ★

Newer Entrepreneur

Isabel recorded her summer business details but didn't fill out her bank *register*. To finish the job, read her record below. Use a calculator to do the *accounting*. Then turn the calculator upside down to see what Isabel plans to buy with her remaining cash.

Sept. 3

Who knew I'd be such an entrepreneur! My business went well this summer, so I've opened a savings account. Since I'm not 18, Mom had to cosign on the account. I endorsed my $600 check on the back to deposit it in my account, and in return, the banker gave me a register to track my money.

Oct. 4

I saw a great sale at Five-Points Plaza. I purchased a skirt for $15 and two sweaters for $15 each. Score!

Oct. 30

I bought three pumpkin cookies at $2.50 each and distributed them to my friends.

Nov. 5

I took Logan to the movies and spent $17.05 on tickets and treats! I didn't go bankrupt, but I should check my balance.

DATE	EXPLANATION	(-) WITHDRAWAL	(+) DEPOSIT	BALANCE
				600.00
9/3	summer business money			600.00
10/4	clothing	45.00		555.00
10/30	cookies	7.50		547.50
11/5	movie tickets and treats	17.05		530.45

What does Isabel plan to buy?

Shoes

Alien Animals

Amber purchased a poster for a new *science-fiction* film, and after staring at it awhile, she realized that the art director had created the creature by combining parts of real animals! Draw a line from each animal part listed to its place on the creature.

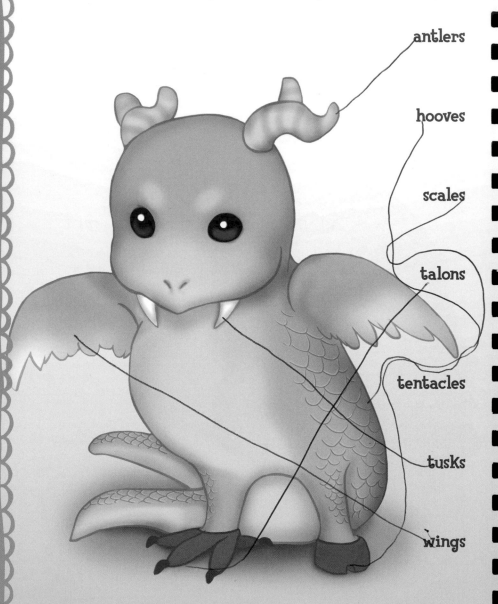

antlers

hooves

scales

talons

tentacles

tusks

wings

By, Buy, Bye!

Homophones are words that sound alike but have different meanings and spellings. If you don't learn those differences, you could write about a "son" in the sky, and your readers will imagine a boy floating on a cloud!

Hear Here

Logan can't believe how often she overhears customers using *homophones* in the bakery. To see this week's batch, place the homophone trios in their correct spots in the sentences. Check out *The Quictionary* if you need help!

1. "So, Mae gave Ms. Stitch her ~~rapt~~ ~~wrapped~~ attention after her teacher ~~rapped~~ ✓ on her desk because Lily had wrapped her shoes in bubble wrap and popped her way to the door!"

    rapped   **rapt**   **wrapped**

2. "I don't mean to err ✓, but I believe our uncle's heir ✓ is outside getting air ✓!"

    air   err   heir

Iced tea $1.50
Chocolate milk $1.50
Vanilla shake $2.50
Berry smoothie $2.75
Peppermint tea $1.25
Hot chocolate $1.50
Café mocha $2.50
Caramel latte $2.75
Chai tea latte $2.50

1. walk your dog today!

2. give your pet a treat

3. A dog is a girl's best friend! ☺

3. "Maya and Sophie, a ___Pair___ ✓ of amazing cooks,

if you ask me, both like to ___pare___ ✓ a

___Pear___ ✓ into their salads."

| pair | pare | pear |

4. "It was such a ___chilly___ ✓ day while we were in

___Chile___ ✓ that we decided to eat a bowl of

___chilly___ ✓ ."

| Chile | chili | chilly |

5. "Then Haley ___rode___ ✓ her bike down the

___road___ ✓ as her friend Kylie ___rowed___ ✓

down the nearby river."

| road | rode | rowed |

Cookie $ .50
Cupcake $1.00
Brownie $ .75
Muffin $1.25
Cake $2.50
Cheesecake $2.75

Double the Fun

Neely gave a homonym crossword puzzle to each of her friends. The puzzles had *exactly* the same answers but completely different definitions! Use one puzzle to help solve the other.

ACROSS

2. Soft, fluffy feathers
4. A written order to a bank
6. A round toy kicked or thrown in a game
7. A wedding ring
9. A layer of paint
10. A river's edge
11. A thick plant stem

DOWN

1. A long skinny rod for fishing or skiing
3. A child's toy that's a cube
4. A hard bandage used to support a bone fracture
5. Nice, generous, and sweet
6. A dog's cry
7. To strike violently
8. A greeting using a hand

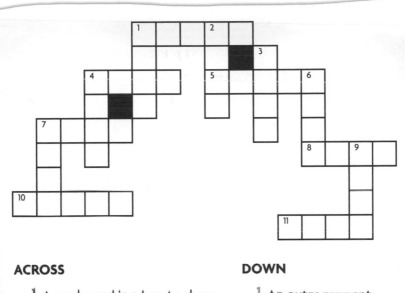

ACROSS

1. A mark used in a box to show something has been done
4. A rhythm in music
5. To secretly follow a person
7. A place where money is kept
8. At a lower level or volume
10. Stop the movement or flow
11. A northern or southern end of the Earth

DOWN

1. An outer garment
2. A group of actors in a play or movie
3. The outer covering on a tree
4. A musical group
6. A group with similar characteristics
7. A fancy party with dancing
9. Curling ocean water

Too Close for Comfort

Isabel used the homophones below incorrectly in her report. Each pair has a difference of only one or two letters, so it was tough for her to recall which was which. Write the letter of the correct word under each object.

1. _____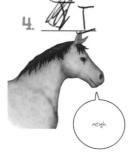

2.  _____

3. _____

4. _____

5. _____

6. F _____

7. _____

8. _____

9. _____

10. H _____

11. _____

12. _____

A. capital

B. capitol

C. flair

D. flare

E. hoarse

F. horse

G. poor

H. pour

I. stationary

J. stationery

K. wail

L. whale

Onyms Island

Onym is a Greek combining form for "name." So words that end in "onym" involve names. For example, synonyms are names with similar meanings. And antonyms are "anti-names," or opposites.

Giggles and Groans

While in the campus cafeteria, Shelby tried telling a few jokes to Paige, but before she could say the punch lines, a friend always walked by chatting about a subject—and using several *synonyms* about that subject! To see Shelby's punch lines, follow the directions.

1. "Why wasn't there any food left after the Halloween party?"
To find out, cross out all the synonyms for "scary" that Isabel used.

creepy because eerie everyone ghastly chilling spooky was a goblin!

2. "What does an octopus wear in the winter?"
To find out, cross out all the synonyms for "laugh" that Amber used.

a chortle coat of guffaw chuckle giggle arms howl

3. "What do you get when you cross a fox with a kangaroo?"
To find out, cross out all the synonyms for "friend" that Riley used.

**crony a ally buddy fur colleague coat mate with
companion a pal pocket sidekick**

4. "After Allison's teacher scolded her for forgetting her homework,
what did Allison reply?"
To find out, cross out all the synonyms for "smart" that Allison used.

**wise why genius get bright angry at me clever for whiz something
astute I didn't brilliant do?**

Camp Weak

Riley found a flyer by her door for a sports camp. Logan read the flyer aloud, replacing certain words with their *antonyms*. The girls cracked up at the results. Replace the highlighted words with their opposites to see what was so funny!

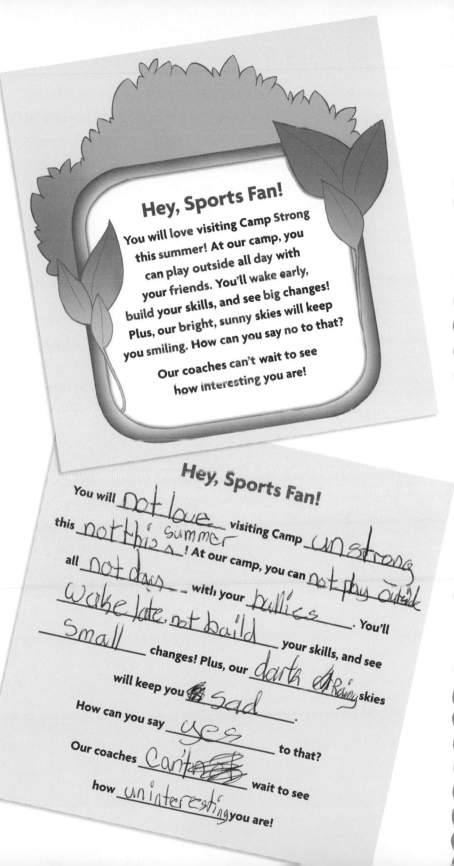

Hey, Sports Fan!

You will love visiting Camp Strong this summer! At our camp, you can play outside all day with your friends. You'll wake early, build your skills, and see big changes! Plus, our bright, sunny skies will keep you smiling. How can you say no to that?

Our coaches can't wait to see how interesting you are!

Hey, Sports Fan!

You will _not love_ visiting Camp _unstrong_ this _not this_ summer _a_! At our camp, you can _not play outside_ all _not days_ with your _bullies_. You'll _wake late, not build_ your skills, and see _small_ changes! Plus, our _dark & Rainy_ skies will keep you _sad_. How can you say _yes_ to that?

Our coaches _Can't_ wait to see how _uninteresting_ you are!

Logan's Letter

Using antonyms was so funny, Logan tried again with a letter from Riley's aunt. "Love" became "hate," and "right" became very "wrong." Unfortunately, Riley's visiting aunt heard every word! To apologize, Logan created this puzzle. Look for the antonyms to the words listed below, and circle them in the word search.

Riley, please tell your aunt that I'm feeling the opposite of these words:

CAREFUL	HOPE	JOY	SUNNY
CHEERFUL	INNOCENT	PUBLIC	WISE
GLAD		RIGHT	

D	E	A	R	R	I	L	E	Y	P
L	Y	D	U	O	L	C	E	W	A
S	H	E	E	F	O	R	S	R	S
G	I	S	T	V	E	S	M	O	E
F	O	P	I	A	E	R	R	N	E
M	B	A	A	L	V	R	R	G	R
A	S	I	E	S	O	I	L	I	N
G	Y	R	O	W	S	O	R	R	Y
U	A	I	N	F	O	R	F	P	O
C	N	T	O	M	F	Y	O	U	R
A	U	N	Y	T	L	I	U	G	T

Secret Sorry

As a special apology to Riley, Logan placed a secret message in her puzzle. To reveal it, write down every letter not circled in the word search at left, reading from left to right and top to bottom.

Ta-Ta Tautonyms

Paige tends to call her friends by *tautonyms*, such as Nee-Nee or Em-Em. A tautonym is a word made up of two matching parts. Can you figure out these other tautonyms?

Small Talk

1. A child might call a minor injury a

   ___ ___ ___ - ___ ___ ___.

2. This toy goes up and down and up and down on a string:

   ___ ___ - ___ ___.

3. Babbling baby talk sounds like . . .

   ___ ___ ___ - ___ ___ ___ and ___ ___ ___ ___.

4. A child might call a train a

   ___ ___ ___ ___ - ___ ___ ___ ___.

Let's Dance

5. Ballet dancers wear a

   ___ ___ ___ ___.

6. A cheerleader might shake a

   ___ ___ ___ - ___ ___ ___.

7. This Latin American ballroom dance uses fast, small steps:

   ___ ___ ___ - ___ ___ ___.

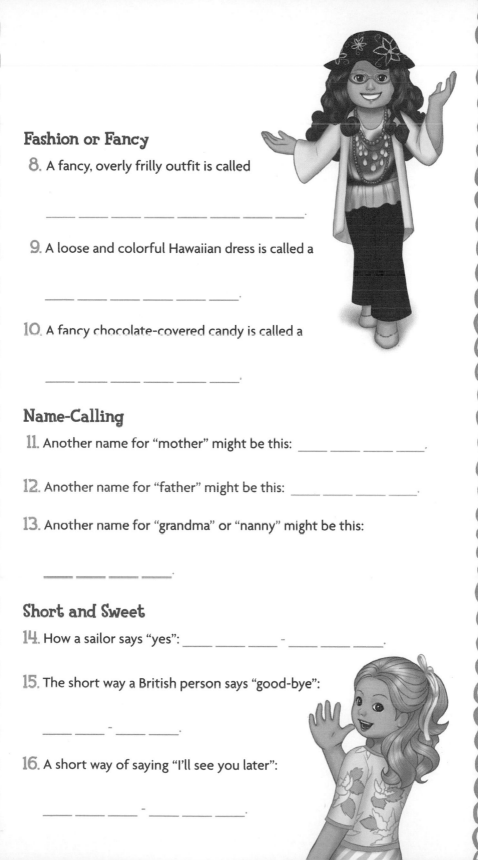

Fashion or Fancy

8. A fancy, overly frilly outfit is called

 ___ ___ ___ ___ ___ ___.

9. A loose and colorful Hawaiian dress is called a

 ___ ___ ___ ___ ___ ___.

10. A fancy chocolate-covered candy is called a

 ___ ___ ___ ___ ___ ___.

Name-Calling

11. Another name for "mother" might be this: ___ ___ ___ ___.

12. Another name for "father" might be this: ___ ___ ___ ___.

13. Another name for "grandma" or "nanny" might be this:

 ___ ___ ___.

Short and Sweet

14. How a sailor says "yes": ___ ___ ___ - ___ ___ ___.

15. The short way a British person says "good-bye":

 ___ ___ - ___ ___.

16. A short way of saying "I'll see you later":

 ___ ___ ___ - ___ ___.

C U at ISU!

Shelby had to take a test on *acronyms, initialisms,* and *abbreviations* so that she could guide guests around campus. Read the definitions below, and then grade Shelby's test on the next page. Place a C beside each correct answer on her test and an I beside each incorrect one. Shelby has to get at least 50 percent correct to get the job. Did she pass?

Acronym (AC)

To make an acronym, you take the first letter from each word in a series, and then pronounce those first letters as their own word. For example, "self-contained underwater breathing apparatus" becomes "scuba."

Intialism (IN)

For an initialism, you take the first letter from each word in a series, and then pronounce those letters as letters. For example, if you shorten "orange juice" to "OJ," when you read it, you pronounce it as "oh-jay." You use initialisms a lot for texting.

Abbreviation (AB)

All shortened words are abbreviations—so acronyms and initialisms are abbreviations—but for this test, an abbreviation is only when you shorten a word, and then you pronounce it as its full word. For example, you might abbreviate "doctor" as "Dr.," but you still say "doctor" when you read it!

ISU DIGNITARY-GUIDE EXAM

C/I	WORD	AC	IN	AB
	STUDENT APPLICANT: _____ Shelby _____			
	1. **Radar** (radio detection and ranging)	✓		
	2. **PIN** (personal identification number)		✓	
	3. **Pop.** (population)			✓
	4. **FYI** (for your information)		✓	
	5. **DVD** (digital video disc)		✓	
	6. **PB&J** (peanut butter & jelly)	✓		
	7. **Jr.** (junior)	✓		
	8. **LOL** (laugh out loud)		✓	
	9. **TTYL** (talk to you later)		✓	
	10. **Dept.** (department)			✓
	11. **DIY** (do-it-yourself)		✓	
	12. **RN** (registered nurse)		✓	
	13. **BFF** (best friends forever)		✓	
	14. **BBQ** (barbecue)	✓		
	15. **SWAT** (special weapons and tactics)	✓		
	16. **U.S.** (United States)		✓	
	Applicant Score:			

Retro Lingo

Logan learned a word so fascinating that she had to tell her friends about it. "A *retronym*," she said, "is when a word must take on an adjective because of an invention." After everyone gave her a ho-hum look, she added, "For example, *hot* was added to *chocolate* after they invented chocolate bars. Before that, all chocolate was hot chocolate!" Connect these retronyms.

Added adjective	Original word
acoustic	diaper
bar	glasses
black-and-white	guitar
cloth	milk
cloth	movie
English	muffin
eye	napkin
hand	pool
inground	restaurant
pocket	skiing
silent	soap
sit-down	television
snow	watch
whole	written

School Studies

Teachers like to sneak vocabulary into their lesson plans. You might be figuring out math problems, but before you know it, you understand the meaning of "diagonal."

Front Office

On the first day of school, the office staff handed Neely notes on where to take new students. Since she's not so great with maps, show Neely her path through the hallways of each building.

Computer Lab

Painting Studio

Pottery Studio

Entry

Help Neely take Leah to the room for creating a picture.

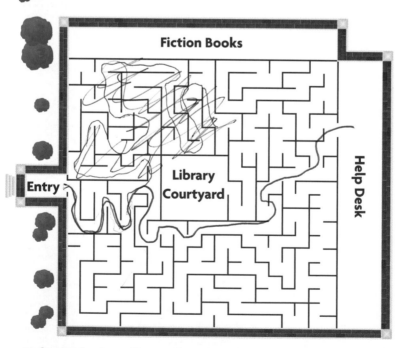

Fiction Books

Library Courtyard

Help Desk

Entry

Help Neely show Sienna the spot to get assistance at the library.

Party Place

Cafeteria

Sweet Treats Bakery

Entry

Help Neely escort Emma to the dining area.

Social Studies: Part 1

Logan's teacher, Ms. Ing, was called away to deal with an emergency. Before leaving, she asked Logan to add the words on the board to her lecture and then read it to the class. The other students will arrive at any minute. Can you help?

citizen
civil war
explorers
famine
government
liberty
president
rural
taxes
urban

When early (1) explorers traveled to new lands, they did so for many reasons. Some were seeking freedom, also called (2) liberty. Some were fleeing an extreme shortage of food, known as a (3) famine. And some were hoping to establish a new country.

When the United States was formed, its leaders created a democracy, a form of (4) government in which citizens elected representatives to manage the nation on their behalf. They also elected a leader, called the (5) President. The country had to decide how much each citizen and business would pay as (6) taxes to support that government.

If a person is born in the United States or chooses to become a member of the U.S., he or she is called a (7) citizen. That person can choose to live in a (8) rural area away from any town or city or an (9) urban area near a town or city. When people within the U.S. split over how things should be done, they battled each other in a (10) Civil war.

Social Studies: Part 2

Then Ms. Ing asked Logan to pass out a cross grid that highlighted the words from her lecture. But first Logan needed to fit each word into the grid herself so that she could check the students' papers. Can you do it for her?

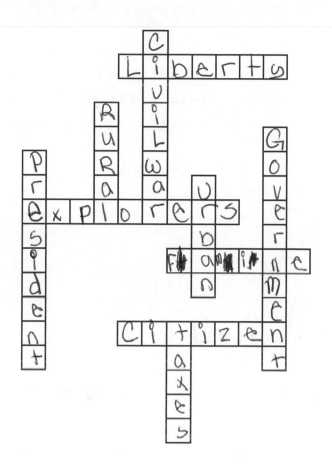

5 letters

RURAL

TAXES

URBAN

6 letters

FAMINE

7 letters

CITIZEN

LIBERTY

8 letters

CIVIL WAR

9 letters

EXPLORERS

PRESIDENT

10 letters

GOVERNMENT

Language Arts

Mr. Ree loves mysteries! He gave his English class a list of definitions related to writing. Write in the word being defined. Then at the bottom, explain how you figured out each word.

Bound opus of knowledge:

_____

Planned layout often thickens:

_____

False and brief legendary events:

_____

Narrative of virtually every length:

_____

Surroundings evoke tantalizing times, including naming geography:

_____

Fun, imaginary compositions that inspire one's notions:

_____

How did you figure out the words being defined?

_____

Art 101

**Read the couplets to help you unscramble
the art terms inside the paint palette.**

1. With your soft bristles,
   we create
   Strokes of color—
   curved and straight.

2. You give support with
   legs of three
   So we can paint the
   things we see.

3. With crayon, pencil,
   ink, or pen,
   We visualize who, what,
   where, or when.

4. This stretched fabric helps
   my paint flow
   So that I can create like
   Vincent van Gogh.

UHSSREB
_____

SLEAE
_____

WINRAGD
_____

SAANVC
_____

Math: Part 1

Ms. Count believes identifying an object is easy if you have a way to recall it. Write the number of the object in the classroom that is similar to each definition. Then turn the page.

_3_ **bar graph**: a diagram that compares things using high and low bars

_2_ **cube**: a three-dimensional box shape with six equal sides

_4_ **Möbius strip**: a surface on a ringed strip with a continuous side

_1_ **pie chart**: a chart that divides a circle into "slices" to compare each slice against the whole circle

_5_ **sphere**: a perfectly round solid circle, such as a ball

1.

2.

3.

4.

5.

Math: Part 2

Did Ms. Count's method work? Remember the object that described each word below, and try to draw its basic shape.

bar graph

cube

Möbius strip

pie chart

sphere

Sounds Like Onomatopoeia

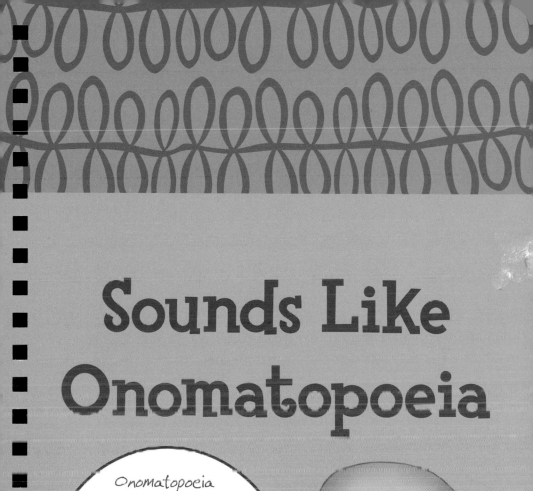

Onomatopoeia (on-oh-mot-oh-pee-ah) means using words that imitate the sounds they describe. Knowing their meanings can improve your stories, poetry, and other creative writing!

Ahem, Action!

Neely shot a cooking-demonstration film for her art class, but she didn't expect so much action! Now, she needs to add sound effects. Read each sound listed at right, and next to it, write the number of the action making that noise.

Cackle Cards

Amber and Shelby are designing cards for a craft sale. Shelby drew animals on the cards, and Amber listed their sounds. Now write each sound on the card of the animal that fits it best.

caw
cluck
cock-a-doodle-doo
coo
croak

gobble
hee-haw
hiss
honk
hoot

howl
roar
squawk
squeak
tweet

Ouch!

Emmy got soap in her eyes while washing bikes for a charity, so Riley took her to the nurse's office. Emmy couldn't see what was happening, but she could guess by the sounds. Read each sound listed below right, and next to it write the number of the patient making that sound.

1 achoo   8 hiccup   6 shush
5 boohoo   2 ouch   4 slurp
3 brrr   9 scratch   7 sniff

Pitter-Patter Pets

Pet Palooza didn't have enough sitters, so Amber brought home a few furry favorites—only now they're keeping her awake! Read each noise listed at right, and next to it, write the number of the animal making that noise.

___ chomp
___ crackle, crackle
___ crash
___ creak, creak
___ plunk, plunk
___ snore
___ squeak, squeak
___ tinkle, tinkle
___ whomp
___ woof

Clatter Control

Every year Neely sends her grandmother a toy to remind her that she's still young at heart. But this year, her grandma requested a silent gift. Read each noise listed below, and next to it write the number of the toy making it. Isabel will send the one that's left.

___ clang, clang
___ clippety-clop
___ ka-ching

___ rattle, rattle
___ squirt, squirt
___ tap, tap, tap

___ twang
___ vroom

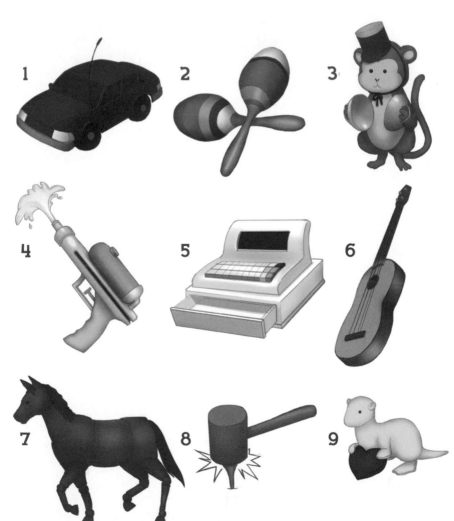

1

2

3

4

5

6

7

8

9

Brilliant
Briticisms

Briticisms are words common to England, Scotland, and Wales. The joy of learning Briticisms is that it's like learning a new language—and that language is English!

Needed: Baby-Minder

While visiting a cousin in London, Logan saw a "Help Wanted" notice on the community bulletin board. She highlighted the words that she didn't understand. Write each highlighted word or term next to the American meaning.

Baby-Minder Needed!

Weekend helper needed in my flat to tend to twins. I have pushchairs and dummies for park trips. The children love cuddly toys and boo-boo plasters. Must be able to change nappies. The twins take afternoon kips in their cots. They're full of beans but a joy! Flat 8B.

Ta, "The Mum."

In an emergency call 999

ROOM TO LET! SEE FLAT 4B

Lost cat! tel: 0011

adhesive bandages: _____

apartment: _____

babysitter: _____

cribs: _____

diapers: _____

mom: _____

naps: _____

pacifiers: _____

strollers: _____

stuffed animals: _____

thank you: _____

very energetic: _____

Nice Nosh-Up

Logan took the baby-minder job, but the Friday before her first day of work, her employer called with a message. Again, she wasn't sure what was said, but it sounded fun! Write each highlighted word next to its American meaning.

Hi, Logan. It's Emma. Can you come to a **nosh-up** tonight at eight? We're serving **chipolatas**, **jacket potatoes**, **aubergines**, and **courgettes** with **coriander**. It'll be a **smashing** time. **Cheerio**.

baked potatoes:

_____

cilantro:

_____

eggplant:

_____

good-bye:

_____

large meal:

_____

small sausages:

_____

very good:

_____

zucchinis:

_____

Sleep Gear

Because Logan's cousin had to leave for class, she asked Logan to gather the remaining things they would need for an upcoming slumber party. Using her cousin's list, match the items at right with their names below.

5 biscuits
1 chips
3 crisps
13 draughts
12 dressing gowns
15 fairy bread
4 fizzies
9 flannels

11 hairgrips
11 hair slides
2 ice lollies
14 jimjams
8 puddings
7 rock cakes
16 sarnies
6 torches

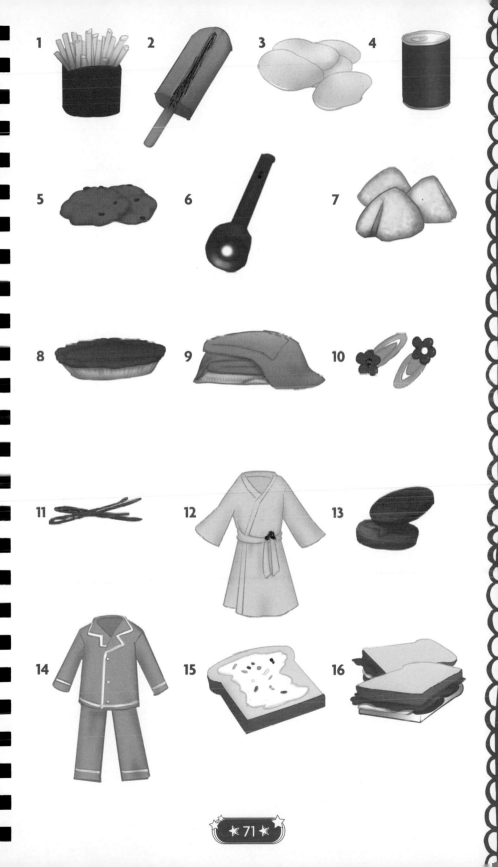

Answers

Craft Laughs
Page 12

1. varnish; 2. embroidery floss;
3. collage; 4. crocheters

Sew Blue
Page 13

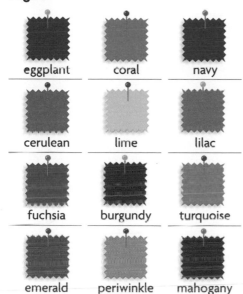

eggplant | coral | navy
cerulean | lime | lilac
fuchsia | burgundy | turquoise
emerald | periwinkle | mahogany

Sorts of Sports
Pages 14–15

1. dismount; 2. barre; 3. infield;
4. shuttlecock; 5. putter;
6. powder; 7. love; 8. hurdles;
9. spinnaker; 10. goggles;
11. épée; 12. goalkeeper

Dress for Dance
Pages 16–17

1. ball gown; 2. tap shoes;
3. unitard; 4. tutu; 5. petticoat;
6. pointe shoes; 7. leotard;
8. ghillies

Earth Art
Page 18
1. B—oxygen; 2. C—recycle;
3. A—repurpose; 4. D—endangered

Bed Boutique
Page 19

A. Bedding dust ruffles; duvets; shams	B. Dresses muumuus; sarongs; shifts
C. Pants capris; chinos; khakis	D. Shirts camisoles; halters; polos
E. Shoes loafers; Mary Janes; mules; platforms	F. Sweaters cardigans; shrugs

Cooking Clues
Page 20

Logan will be serving PASTA.

Music Mania
Page 21

1. E; 2. D; 3. A; 4. B; 5. F; 6. C

Twisted Travelogue
Pages 22–23

Paige's luggage didn't arrive on her flight. She'll take a gondola to a hotel in Italy.

Newer Entrepreneur
Pages 24–25

Isabel has $530.45 left, and her next purchase will be shoes!

DATE	EXPLANATION	(-) WITHDRAWAL	(+) DEPOSIT	BALANCE
9/3	summer business money		600.00	600.00
10/4	clothing	45.00		555.00
10/30	cookies	7.50		547.50
11/5	movie tickets and treats	17.05		530.45

Alien Animals
Page 26

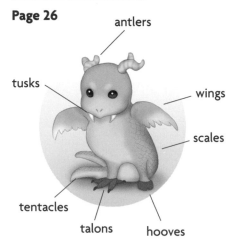

antlers

tusks

wings

scales

tentacles

talons

hooves

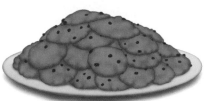

Hear Here
Pages 28–29

1. rapt, rapped, wrapped
2. err, heir, air
3. pair, pare, pear
4. chilly, Chile, chili
5. rode, road, rowed

Double the Fun
Pages 30–31

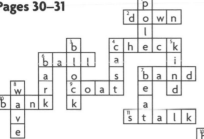

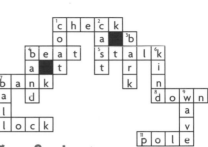

Too Close for Comfort
Page 32

1. I; 2. A; 3. D; 4. J; 5. C; 6. F; 7. E;
8. B; 9. L; 10. H; 11. K; 12. G

neigh

Giggles and Groans
Pages 34–35

1. Because everyone was a goblin!
2. A coat of arms
3. A fur coat with a pocket
4. Why get angry at me for something I didn't do?

Camp Weak
Pages 36–37

Hey, Sports Fan!

You will hate visiting Camp Weak
this winter! At our camp, you
can work inside all night with
your enemies. You'll sleep late,
destroy your skills, and see little
changes! Plus, our dark, cloudy skies
will keep you frowning.
How can you say yes to that?
Our coaches can wait to see
how boring you are!

Logan's Letter
Page 38

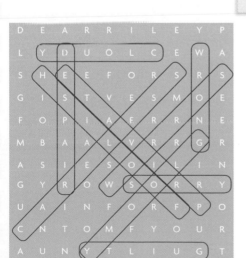

Secret Sorry
Page 39

Dear Riley,
Please forgive me for embarrassing
you in front of your aunt.

Ta-Ta Tautonyms

Pages 40–41

1. boo-boo; 2. yo-yo;
3. goo-goo and gaga; 4. choo-choo;
5. tutu; 6. pom-pom; 7. cha-cha;
8. froufrou; 9. muumuu; 10. bonbon;
11. mama; 12. papa; 13. nana;
14. aye-aye; 15. ta-ta; 16. bye-bye

C U at ISU!

Pages 42–43

1. C; 2. I (PIN is an acronym and is pronounced as "pin"); 3. C; 4. C; 5. C; 6. I (PB&J is an initialism since you say each letter); 7. I (This is an abbreviation because you read "Jr." as "junior"); 8. C; 9. C; 10. C; 11. C; 12. C; 13. C; 14. I (This is an abbreviation because you read "BBQ" as "barbecue"); 15. C; 16. C; Shelby passed the test. She missed 4 out of 16, so she got 75% correct!

Retro Lingo

Page 44

acoustic guitar: Electric guitars caused this retronym.

bar soap: Before liquid soap, most soap was made into a solid bar.

black-and-white television: Even after color TVs were invented, it took a while for black-and-white TVs to disappear.

cloth diaper: Disposable diapers made this a retronym.

cloth napkin: Paper napkins initiated this change.

English muffin: To distinguish this muffin from the sweet cupcake-like pastries, its name had to change.

eyeglasses: Can you guess what invention changed this word? Sunglasses!

handwritten: Typewriters caused this retronym.

inground pool: All swimming pools were inground until above-ground pools splashed onto the scene.

pocket watch: People kept all watches in their pockets—until they wore them on their wrists! Many pants still include the watch pocket!

silent movie: "Talkies" caused movies to take a "silent" partner.

sit-down restaurant: This recent retronym came about to distinguish a restaurant with waitstaff from fast-food restaurants.

snow skiing: All skiing was in the snow until people slid their skis into the water.

whole milk: This word came along after manufacturers reduced milk's fat content.

Front Office

Pages 46–47

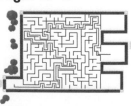
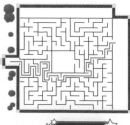
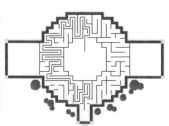

Social Studies: Part 1
Pages 48–49

1. explorers; 2. liberty; 3. famine;
4. government; 5. president; 6. taxes;
7. citizen; 8. rural; 9. urban; 10. civil war

Language Arts
Page 52

1. book; 2. plot; 3. fable; 4. novel;
5. setting; 6. fiction
You can find the word being defined
by reading the first letter of each word.

Art 101
Page 53

1. brushes; 2. easel; 3. drawing; 4. canvas

Math: Part 1
Pages 54–55

1. pie chart; 2. cube; 3. bar graph;
4. Möbius strip; 5. sphere

Math: Part 2
Page 56

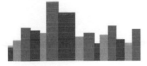

bar graph

cube

Möbius strip

sphere

pie chart

*Turn the page for the
answers to pages 60–61.*

Social Studies: Part 2
Pages 50–51

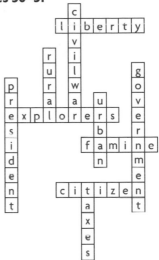

Ahem, Action!
Pages 58–59

9 clink
3 fizz
6 sizzle
5 tap, tap
4 ticktock

8 whack
1 whir
2 whiz
7 yip

Ouch!
Pages 62–63

1 achoo
5 boohoo
3 brrr

8 hiccup
2 ouch
9 scratch

6 shush
4 slurp
7 sniff

Pitter-Patter Pets

Pages 64–65

_9_ chomp
_10_ crackle, crackle
_2_ crash
_6_ creak, creak
_5_ plunk, plunk

_8_ snore
_3_ squeak, squeak
_1_ tinkle, tinkle
_7_ whomp
_4_ woof

Clatter Control

Page 66

_3_ clang, clang
_7_ clippety-clop
_5_ ka-ching
_2_ rattle, rattle

_4_ squirt, squirt
_8_ tap, tap, tap
_6_ twang
_1_ vroom

Neely sent a stuffed animal.

Needed: Baby-Minder

Page 68

adhesive bandages: _plasters_
apartment: _flat_
babysitter: _baby-minder_
cribs: _cots_
diapers: _nappies_
mom: _mum_
naps: _kips_
pacifiers: _dummies_
strollers: _pushchairs_
stuffed animals: _cuddly toys_
thank you: _ta_
very energetic: _full of beans_

Nice Nosh-Up

Page 69

baked potatoes: _jacket potatoes_
cilantro: _coriander_
eggplant: _aubergines_
good-bye: _cheerio_
large meal: _nosh-up_
small sausages: _chipolatas_
very good: _smashing_
zucchinis: _courgettes_

Cackle Cards

Pages 60–61

Sleep Gear

Pages 70–71

_5_ biscuits
_1_ chips
_3_ crisps
_13_ draughts
_12_ dressing gowns
_15_ fairy bread
_4_ fizzies
_9_ flannels
_11_ hairgrips
_10_ hair slides
_2_ ice lollies
_14_ jimjams

_8_ puddings
_7_ rock cakes
_16_ sarnies
_6_ torches

INNERSTARU.com

The puzzle fun continues online!

Use the code below for access to
even more puzzles and activities.

Go online to innerstarU.com/puzzle
and enter this code: AGIRLSWORD

Basic System Requirements:
Windows: Internet Explorer 7 or 8, Firefox 2.0+, Google Chrome
Mac: Safari 4.0+
Monitor Resolution: Optimized for 1024 x 768 or larger
Flash Version 10 and high-speed Internet required

Requirements may change. Visit www.innerstarU.com for
full requirements and latest updates.

Important Information:
Recommended for girls 8 and up. American Girl reserves the right
to modify, restrict access to, or discontinue www.innerstarU.com
at any time, in its sole discretion, without prior notice.

Flash!
Pull out the flash cards in the
back of the book, fill them in,
and see how quickly you learn
new words!

Here are some other American Girl books you might like: